YOU ARE THE MAGIC

DOUGLAS MYRICK

with LaRanda L. Phillips

YOU ARE
THE MAGIC

DOUGLAS MYRICK

with LaRanda L. Phillips

First Printing, 2016

ISBN-13: 978-1540562036

ISBN-10: 1540562034

AromaNetix

www.AromaNetix.com

DEDICATION

Sincere and heartfelt thanks to my family and friends,
whose support and encouragement have been instrumental
in this work. Thank you so very much!

This book is likewise dedicated to the thinking individual
searching for encouragement and greater meaning to it all.
Life is meant to be experienced on every level.
May you find in these pages a few morsels for your journey.

Special thanks to LaRanda L. Phillips for her tireless research
gathering these and other quotes of mine,
stretching back over six years of social media.

For my friend, James Lewis.
I finally saw the ocean!

FOREWORD

Thank you for reading this book.
The following quotes are a selection from many hundreds
of my social media posts spanning over six years' time.

Much like a buffet, there is something for everyone.
If something resonates with you, that is wonderful;
discard any ideas that are not in harmony with your beliefs.
Does that sound fair enough?

There truly is something special inside of you!
May you find within this book a few nuggets
of useful philosophical "gold" and remember
that the magic is within you.

To your success!

Douglas Myrick
Creator of AromaNetix

You

truly

are the

Magic.

Live
Largely.

There will never
be another
now.

Just because you can't doesn't mean you shouldn't.

You can learn a lot from attempting the unlikely, and who knows...you just might win.

The scope of your vision determines your future.

Place more dreams in your life and you shall add more life to your dreams.

When did we begin to allow the pain of the past to dictate our reality?

When did we stop jumping out of bed at 5:30 AM, impatiently waiting for Saturday morning cartoons to begin? When did Christmas morning start to lose its innocent, childlike magic? When did we stop saying "and a half" when telling our age?

We are timeless, eternal
beings of purest
love and energy.

We do not truly die, so
why not do something
spectacular with your
eternity?

Go For It!

Let go.

Act on your intuitive impulses and allow the results to manifest. Be willing to be pleasantly surprised by a loving, magical universe.

Abundance is
your birthright.

Accept it. Embrace it.

You need not
struggle in life.

*I am come that they might have
life, and that they might
have it more abundantly.*
— (KJV) John 10:10

Someone
somewhere loves
you just for who
you are.

Walk in
that flow.

Expect a miracle.

There is authentic magic
in believing.
Feel free to reach out
and claim it, because your
wish has already been
given to you.

Open yourself to the
undeniable majesty
surrounding you
at each moment.

The Universe is
within you, closer than
your next breath.

Believe.

There is a solution.

Do not look harder;
instead, look away
and listen.

Are you struggling
for what you want?

Why do as
everyone else does?

Don't dig for the gold;
sell the shovels.

To *want* something actually
means to lack it.
Whenever you constantly
reaffirm that you *want*
something, what you are saying
is that you *lack* it.

As such, you continue to lack it.

If you desire something,
claim it in the NOW:
*"I'm experiencing this,
and I'm so glad!"*

Life is a gift.
Savor its rewards!

If you desire more
abundance, create it!
You are good enough
just as you are.

Discover the free path
and explore your juicy,
unforgettable life.

Your natural, limitless ability is reflected in the beauty of every waking moment.

Enjoy what you are and reach for even higher ground.

I believe in you.

Experience is watching someone swing repeatedly at nothing but air, meanwhile the *piñata* waits just a few feet to the right, ready to reveal countless treasures.

You're working hard enough; just shift your direction.

You're good enough
to handle it.
You're strong enough.
Smart enough.

Today is another
chance to
prove it
to yourself.

Live with passion, even though you're hurting. Persist.

Character is the high water mark left when the floods of life recede.

It's simple
to teach what was
difficult
to
learn.

The fastest way to lift up
from depression is
to go help someone
who cannot repay you.

Your mind cannot hold
two simultaneous,
conflicting opinions
of your value
to the world.

Be the difference.

You may live to reach
100, but you will
inhabit a 100
year old body.

Get out there now and
create some
breathtaking memories
to savor during your
golden years.

Right now someone
you know is hurting,
inside. Find them
and be a light for
them in troubled times.

The torch you hold
may help them make it
through the night.

It only takes one to
start a transformation.

In a world of sorrow,
you can be that
spark of light.

Deep-seated feelings of unworthiness will hold you back from receiving blessings and abundance.

When you help those less fortunate you silence those tired, old ghosts from the past.

Break Free.
You can.

You have more power
than you realize.
Walk in harmony with
the greatness within.

Look inside and
remember the good you
have done for others.
Those tender moments
are the love of God,
expressed.

One purpose of human
existence is to bring the
spirit of loving kindness
to this world.

In truth, it is the Light of
all lights, and the true
Source of First Cause.

Breathe.
Feel.
Be.
Love.

Sometimes instead of eating lunch I'll give the money/food to someone in greater need.

My brief period of hunger reminds me to more deeply recognize both the day-to-day struggles of others and the blessings I enjoy.

Stay real.

We are timeless
consciousness
wrapped around a
mortal frame.

Take heart!
Show love.
Embody compassion.

All are one.
One is all.

A mind at ease and a tranquil countenance are the priceless rewards of peaceful service.

That which we give, we get.

Opportunity
will not wait
for the
unprepared.

Find a dream.
Learn the price.
Create a plan.

Work like it matters.

Spoil yourself
and the universe
corresponds
to the nature
of your bliss.

What you give
yourself
reveals yourself.
Be fabulous.

I played grocery store with
little Oliver and he asked me
"what would you like today?"

I laughed and answered
"world peace and a
stack of $100's".

Without hesitation, he smiled
and handed me my order.

Children don't
lack understanding.

We lack belief.

There was a great bonfire,
with countless sparks
leaping into the night.

A spark can quickly
spread the work
of its source.

So may we spread
understanding,
compassion,
tenderness,
and hope.

There was a simple man who used his shovel like a hammer. All day long he worked and worked, yet little was accomplished.

Are you using
your tools correctly?

Often the answer
isn't greater effort,
but greater
understanding.

The imagination is more than a playground for thoughts; it is the forge where dreams take shape.

Use it very often and believe.

Your creative mind
has the ability to
conceive any
worthwhile destiny
that you desire.

First, believe yourself
worthy to have the life
of your dreams.

When the going gets tough...quit.

Quit doing it the hard way.
Quit blaming others.
Quit doing it all yourself.
Quit beating yourself up.

Quit feeling guilty.
Quit taking so much crap.
Quit saying yes all the time.
Quit apologizing so much.
Quit needing permission.

Quit reading this. Go WIN!

Do not despise fear and worry, for they remind us that we are coming into alignment with our true, authentic purpose.

One day I picked up a
swatter and chased a fly
through the kitchen.

The fly landed directly on
the swatter and stared at me
for over a minute.

I opened the door
and set the fly free.

Courage
changes
outcome.

When you lead
your life
with love,
you'll love the
life you lead.

Looking for your
life's purpose?

The chalkboard is clear.

You are always
free to design
your own mission.

BREAKING NEWS:
You are loved
just as you are.

Deeply.
Truly.

Build upon that.

How to let go of the past:

1. Reduce what hurts.
2. Release the blame.
3. Redefine the lesson.

You are
worthy of greater
experiences,
rich relationships,
and meaningful
satisfaction.

It is already yours!

A simple shift in focus
brings you to the light.

Today
is
another chance
to get it
right.

If you focus continually
on the negative news
you may miss the subtle
blessings at your feet.

What you focus upon
with strong emotion
directs your attitude, your
actions and your future.

Choose wisely.

There is more
than enough
for you.

Ask.

God didn't go to all this
trouble for you to lead
an ordinary life.

Persistence:

It takes most people a
year to learn to walk,
falling time and
time again.

Many people give up on
their dreams by the third
or fourth rejection.

Get up.
Try again.

There is a boundless universe within each person, filled with pure potentiality.

Explore the breathtaking cosmos within when you need a refreshing break.

So often we forget that
earthly life is no more
permanent than a few weeks
away at summer camp.
We came from another
place, and there
we shall return.

To desire to *leave one's mark*
upon this world is fine, but
only as meaningful as
carved initials on the camp
picnic table.

There is
a part of you
that
never surrenders.

Begin there.

Your amazing body
has a genetic blueprint
locked in each cell.

That blueprint allowed
you to develop and grow.

Listen. Release.
Renew. Rejuvenate.

Your body has the map.
It knows the way back.

She looked inside
the tattered,
smudged container
and discovered a
diamond of
inestimable worth; a
pearl of great price; a
gold most pure.

She looked within.
She found herself.

You, my friend, are greatness. I believe in you.

There is a nagging voice of self-criticism that wants you to feel powerless; pay it absolutely no attention.

When you silence the frightened inner critic you'll see the truth:

You are truly special!

"If self-help
really worked you'd
only need to use
it once" muttered
the man on his
way to take a shower.

Once you see
what you are
underneath what
you seem,
life becomes blessed;
a dream
within a dream!

I love to leave a
quarter in the
gumball machine.

Really, it costs
so little to make
someone's day.

There was a woman who phoned in a song request to a radio station, but she forgot to turn on her radio.
Her request was answered, but she missed hearing her song.

There are no unanswered prayers, only conditions that block our ability to receive.

Whenever I meet
someone the first time I
mentally say to them,
"I respect you."

If more people began
in this manner we
would achieve greater
unity and peace
in twenty-four hours.

I respect you.

People are like
rays of pure light
extending from
one true Source.

Each person is
capable of greatness.

See them that way
and many will rise
to fulfill your
high expectation.

Do you honestly believe that you deserve more from life?

If your mind holds conflicting beliefs about worthiness or success you may find that it becomes difficult to consistently achieve high results.

AromaNetix can help.

There is a divine Source.
You are a spark from that
divinity, with a purpose
to be fulfilled.

You come from
very special stuff.

Make sure to take a
moment each morning
to remember that
you are royalty.

Feel it.

No mirror ever shines
as brightly as
the one we hold up
for another.

You can be that
gentle inspiration
if you think you can.

Service is a privilege
of the heart.

A stone at the base
of a great mountain is
no less a rock.

You came to Earth
with the loving powers
of Source.
Search for them within.

As above, so below.

At our core, we are
magnificent
spiritual beings.

We are all part of One
consciousness.

We are interconnected
in the perfect fabric
of eternity.

Live fearlessly.

Failure is
temporary.

Failure awakens us
to the lessons of the
moment.

You haven't lost.
You are learning.

Forgiveness
is a
powerful
medicine
for the
soul.

Isn't it time?

"I am 179 years old, and I owe it all to strenuous exercise and a strict diet" said no one ever.

You only live once. Have the pie.

Change is
an opportunity
for advancement.

Embrace it.
Master it.

You just might enjoy it.

Every good and useful
purpose has divinity
for a soul mate.

Let your light shine and
your tribe will find you.

Heart knows heart.

If you've got a dream
worth fighting for,
protect it.
Even if no one else believes
in it, protect it.

If you will walk in certainty
of it, prepare in expectation
for it, and move ahead
despite worldly denials of it,
the Universe will
correspond to the
nature of your actions.

Give yourself a break.

You are much
more on track
than you realize.

Breathe.
Flow.

You can do this.

The best sale
you'll ever make
is the day you
convince yourself
that you were
born to win.

You truly can
have it all,
with peace of mind.

One of the richest men I ever met once said, "Douglas, life isn't real. It is a game, and you'd better start playing. Stop being so serious. It will all work out."

He was right.

I can choose to feel
worthy, generous and
loving.
I receive without guilt,
give without expectation,
and love without fear.

Timelessly onward.

You are always
in alignment with the
Higher Good.

The Universe has
your back.

Show It what you
can do.

There are people
who shape your life in
small, subtle ways that
end up making a big
difference.

They are your tribe.

LIFE can stand for
Learning Immersion
For Enlightenment.

We are here to grow.
We are here to expand.
We are here to experience.

We are here to love.

Let go.

You don't have to
see the whole map.

Just keep moving so the
Captain can steer your
ship safely to harbor.
It will be okay.

Today's affirmation:

"My power is now.
Here, in the present.
I am not my past.
I am not yet my future.
Just for today, in every
way, I shall be in present
focus and present reality.
My power is now."

Give yourself
permission to seek
life without limits, in
whatever form
your heart desires.

Release the guilt and
unworthiness.
You can be trusted
with abundance
in every perfect way.
It's time.

Always remember
that love is the answer.
The world is ready to
give you love when it sees
the love you give.

Go ahead and love again
when you're ready.

It just might be
amazing.

Life is too short
to miss a
single moment.

There will never be
another NOW.

I hope you'll make
each now count.

People are searching
for meaning and purpose
in their lives.

In the history of
humankind there has
never been a greater time
than now for opportunity
and growth.

Beyond *how* is your *what*.
Begin there and you'll
figure out the rest.

Today's focus:

"I can choose to refuse the losing attitudes of negative people."

Your thoughts and
feelings determine the
direction of your life.

It is you who writes
the songs of tomorrow.

Make them extraordinary.

Human evolution
would go faster
if some would
relax their grip
on the past.

Yet, everything
unfolds according
to plan.

Conflicting inner beliefs and values may create obstacles in your life path.

Search your feelings for resistance to your goals, and then clear away those emotional blockages.

Restoration of internal emotional balance can open the way to change.

Motivation is nice,
but take action.

It is the doing of the thing
that yields results.

Take immediate action.

There is little point
in steering a parked car.

Take action.
You can adjust your
strategy as you go.

Decision is a
driving force that
propels you toward
your dreams and goals.

There's nothing quite as
powerful as a dream
backed by a firm decision
that you can do, be, and
have more in this life.

So, decide.

Fear is the enemy
of your dreams.
If no devil existed, fear
would be enough to *bedevil*
the mind of humanity.

An awakened spirit
knows that fear is an
illusion, for what can a
timeless, eternal being ever
truly lose?

Be Free!

Give praise and honor to the divine Source, as you choose to see It.

As you apprehend the beauty and perfection of the All, you draw nearer to that which is good, and so become more like It.

Are you
the
candle
or are you
the flame?

There is a reason
that you are here.
Even if you do not
recall the details, when
the time is right you
will remember the
feeling.

Let your feelings guide
you back to purpose.

There is
within you
a connection
to the Universe
that will last
the test of time.

You need never feel
alone.

Allow your victory.

Struggling?

Take notes along the way,
for you are the teacher of
tomorrow.

People are hungry for the
message that only you
may teach them.

Share your victory!

If you have nothing to invest into your future, offer vulnerability.

When we bare our heart and soul the true value of our intentions appears.

Now is the perfect time to act on your dreams!

Listen, you matter. Your story is NOT over, yet.

Run on my faith for a while, until you believe again!

Do you
remember
what you are?

Not what you
were, but a deeper
reality; a recognition
within that shines.

It is a knowing.

Once you learn
life's harder lessons
you need not
repeat them.

Give yourself
permission to
advance without
repeated hardship.

You have a say.

Decide
to just be yourself.

You will be criticized no
matter what you do.
Please yourself.

There is no shortage of
critics in the world,
but there is only one you.

Heck, you just might
start a trend.

It is your perfect right
to strike a balance in life
when you can.

Examine your life path
and uncover
opportunities for
meaningful growth.

An enriched life is a
shining example to all.

Forgiveness
is a gift
that gives
twice.

Forgive a little
more deeply
when you can.

Compassion
is a soothing balm
in troubled times.

Walk within the
almighty hands of
Source, and then
serve with heart.

We never truly lose
anything forever.

When you feel far from
loved ones, picture them.
Think of them.
Feel them.

They are closer
than your next breath,
loved by Perfect Source
always and in all ways.

When you find yourself
feeling happy,
keep going with that
feeling all day long.

You're attracting into
your life path more
happy experiences.

Try it in belief.

One of the
great mysteries
of life is that
you get a say
in what comes next.

You won't always
get to choose
how it unfolds,
but you do get
to select the topic.

Choose what works
best for you in life.

In the end what matters
most is whether or not
you have learned how to
love your fellow people.

Open up a little more,
when you're ready.

Your perception of reality
is shaped by what you
feed into your mind.

Give it nourishing
thoughts and BIG ideas.

An investment in
your attitude can yield
tremendous dividends.

Don't fight
the change.

Change
the
fight.

There is a miracle coming your way.

Will you accept?

Work with the flow
and opportunities
come into your path.

In college I made
a little money selling
"No Soliciting" signs
door-to-door.

Go with the flow.

A righteous and
loving act
creates waves
of spiritual force
that can quickly
generate impactful
and lasting
changes in the
lives of millions.

Take a chance.

Today
can be the day
that you begin.

Don't worry
about how.

Your victory is
already purchased.

May the
True and
Perfect Source
of all bless you
and keep you,
always and
in all ways.

Walk in love.

There is something
magnificent
about you,
deep down inside,
and it can shine
through when you
allow love in.

When you're ready.

Frustration
is the perceived
inability to
create meaningful
change.

Remove the limiting
perception and
change can begin.

What can we ever truly own?

We come into this world empty handed, needing love and provision.

We go into the next world carrying only love and experience.

At the time of our
renewal we simply pass
into our original state
of pure energy and
pure consciousness.

When we switch off the
radio, does the radio
station disappear?

Take heart.
In the end, life
truly begins.

Love and experiences are all that we may ever truly own.

May your life be abundantly blessed with both, that you may be free and fulfilled beyond measure.

A king hosted a great
scavenger hunt.

Some found trinkets and
amusements, while others
found wealth and
high adventure.

Afterward, each was
rewarded with a splendid
feast and great treasure.

Such is life.
Make your search
extraordinary.

What stands
before you
cannot compare
to what
reigns
within you.

Say the word.
Unleash the power.

Fear
tells us that
we
can't.

The soul
laughs:
just watch me.

Fear is a prison
of ideology.

Love is a
lighthouse
shining through
the darkest night.

Find your way home.

The rigors and
challenges of life
distract you from who
you truly are:
a spark of
God the Source.

You are the magic.

Awaken and remember.

One may dissolve
into the primordial
essence of the All;
to melt away into
the Everything,
as a drop of purest
water in an
endless ocean.

Simply be.

Often it is not
the fear of failure that
stops us, but the fear of
success that holds us
back.

Some of the most
competent professionals
secretly wrestle with the
fear of success.

AromaNetix can help.

There is a rhythm
to the universe.

If you can find a quiet,
contemplative place
within, ask your soul
to guide you to the
harmonic shores
of belief.

Let us meet there.

You are one decision
away from stepping
beyond fear into destiny.

It will test you;
if it doesn't, you are on
the wrong path.

You'll never forget where
you were the moment
you made that
quality decision.

Just get started.

The way will
present itself.

Until you find
your own belief,
lean on the belief of
friends and family.

You absolutely can do it.

If you don't choose
to do it that's okay, too.

The decision is yours.
You don't have to
choose it at this time.

Be willing to give yourself
the gift of time.

Savor the moments
of playful recreation.

Play is so important
because it doesn't just
make you happy now, but
it also creates delicious
memories that can
last a lifetime.

Go out and play.

If you're in a rut,
you're vulnerable to a
blindside from life.
Don't let yourself
stay too comfortable.

Break free.
Because there are bigger
comforts to be had.

Get hungry.
Find a bigger dream.

Recall the magic of
your first kiss?
Blissful anticipation.

You can feel
that way, again.

Discover the power
to release the past, feel
better fast, and totally
transform your life.

Absolutely yes.

You are
the Magic.
Your dreams
are the creative
force that sets it all
into motion.

Dare to believe again.
Dare to dream again.
If you do,
you just might find
the magic still
inside of you.

There is greatness in you waiting to be unleashed.

It hides behind familiarity, habit, routine, and comfort.

When you do the uncomfortable, you awaken the unstoppable.

Compassion
is the love letter you
pass to God
through others.

Make it heart-felt.

Difference
is the unique flavor
that one may add to
the collective recipe of
human existence.

What sets an individual
apart is the ability to
increase value in the lives
of others, and so
improve the recipe.

Be yourself in every wonderful, passion-driven way. For we are introduced by our commonalities, but remembered for our magical differences.

You are loved.
You are needed.

You are good enough.

Hope.

There is something you've been praying about for some time...

...an answer is coming.

Believe.

There is something
that you are still
holding on to
from the past.

It's your business,
not mine,
but, isn't it time
to maybe lay it down?

You've had to be strong
for so long.

You
can be such a blessing
to someone in need
right now.

A smile.
A phone call.
An encouraging letter.

You always have the
power to lift up.

I've never been
so downhearted
that I couldn't
stop to help someone
in worse circumstances.

Uplifting another
is God's secret
medicine for the soul.

If you can lift up,
you can get up.

There is a collective
All that unites
human experiences
into one rhythm.

Breathe and remember.

Take all the time
you need.

The heart-throb of
eternity is yours.

Power
is the ability to
command change.

Take back
your power.

Isn't it time
to create the life
of your dreams?

Every
awakened mind
is a personal victory.

Emotional liberation
is a pathway
to the hidden,
untapped power
residing within you.

Unlcash it.

When you see yourself
as you wish to become
you rally the powers
of Heaven to your cause.

Helpful energies place you
on your true path;
a life path that is
perfectly suited for you.

It's yours to explore.
Are you ready?

A child wandered into a candy shop, only to find no one was there. Behind the counter stood a mirror with a note taped upon it:

The shop belongs to you, now.
Fill your pockets to
overflowing, every day.

Take. Give.
Enjoy. Live.

Precious one, you truly
are the magic.

Blow bubbles
and check out from
adulthood for the
afternoon.

You are the Magic.

Believe
in possibilities.

Your dreams can
come true.

The Universe is
everywhere;
the magic
is in
YOU.

For more information about
AromaNetix visit us online at
<u>AromaNetix.com</u>

Blessings and abundance are yours,
always and in all ways.

- Douglas

Made in the USA
Monee, IL
07 July 2026